October 7, 2009

Withdrawal of U.S. Forces from Iraq: Possible Timelines and Estimated Costs

Summary and Introduction

President Obama has announced that all U.S. combat operations for the war in Iraq—also called Operation Iraqi Freedom (OIF)—will cease by the end of August 2010. According to the timeline described by Administration officials, the approximately 128,000 U.S. military personnel currently in Iraq would remain there through the Iraqi elections scheduled for January 2010. After that, U.S. forces would decline to no more than 50,000 troops by the end of August 2010. In accordance with the Status of the Forces Agreement signed by Iraq and the United States in November 2008, the remaining 50,000 U.S. troops must leave the country by the end of December 2011. The Congressional Budget Office (CBO) estimates that to comply with that timeline, the Administration will need to withdraw military personnel from Iraq in two stages: one between the Iraqi election and August 2010, when almost 80,000 U.S. troops would be removed over a period of seven months, and the other before the end of calendar year 2011, when 50,000 troops will need to be withdrawn.

CBO estimated two broad categories of costs under the Administration's plan and under several alternatives. Some of those costs—which the Department of Defense (DoD) calls operations costs—including incremental military personnel costs attributable to the war in Iraq and costs for fuel, transportation, and maintenance of equipment in Iraq, would decrease proportionately with the number of service members in the country. Such costs, therefore, would be essentially zero by fiscal year 2013 when, under the Administration's plan, no U.S. forces would remain in Iraq. CBO estimated other costs, for activities that DoD labels "equipment reconstitution," that would not decrease proportionately with the number of troops: costs to repair equipment that is used in the war and returned to the United States and costs to replace equipment lost in the conduct of the war. CBO estimates that costs for operations and equipment reconstitution under the Administration's plan would total $51 billion in 2010 and would decline to $3 billion by 2013.

At the request of the Chairman of the Subcommittee on National Security and Foreign Affairs of the House Committee on Oversight and Government Reform, CBO examined several alternative timetables for withdrawal of U.S. forces from Iraq.

Three options would withdraw all U.S. forces before the end of December 2011, as planned by the Administration:

- Option 1 would remove U.S. forces beginning in October 2009 at a rate of 14,400 troops per month to complete the withdrawal by the end of June 2010.

- Option 2 would draw forces down more rapidly—at a rate of 17,500 service members per month—starting in October 2009 and removing all troops by May 2010.

- Option 3 would conduct the withdrawal at the same rate as Option 2—17,500 troops per month—but begin after Iraq's elections, scheduled for January 2010. Under this option, withdrawal would be complete by September 2010.

CBO also examined another plan, Option 4, that would withdraw U.S. troops more slowly and steadily than under the Administration's plan, at a rate of 5,500 service members per month over 23 months beginning after the Iraqi elections, with all troops withdrawn by the end of December 2011.

As it did for the Administration's withdrawal schedule (set to begin after the Iraqi elections in January 2010), CBO identified how some annual costs associated with OIF would change from 2010 through 2014 under the four alternative timetables. CBO estimates that costs over the period from 2009 to 2014 would be $156 billion under the Administration's plan but $50 billion to $54 billion less if troops began to withdraw in October 2009, as they would under Option 1 or Option 2 (see Table 1). The greatest savings would be realized under Option 2, which provides for a faster withdrawal, removing 17,500 troops per month over 8 months. Savings relative to the Administration's plan would be smaller if the withdrawal of U.S. forces from Iraq did not begin until after the elections—approximately $34 billion if troops were withdrawn by September 2010, as called for under Option 3. A more gradual withdrawal CBO analyzed—Option 4—would cost about $5 billion more than the Administration's plan.

CBO did not evaluate the operational or security disadvantages associated with drawing down U.S. forces in Iraq earlier or more rapidly than planned by the Administration. The withdrawal of significant numbers of U.S. military personnel before the Iraqi elections could increase security risks during a time of high tensions in Iraq. And removing U.S. forces and their associated equipment faster than the Administration has planned could place U.S. forces that remain in Iraq at greater risk of attack and result in the buildup of equipment at Kuwaiti ports awaiting shipment to the United States or at U.S. ports awaiting transportation to bases in the United States.

Table 1.

Military Personnel and Costs of Operations and Equipment Reconstitution in OIF Under the Administration's Plan and Alternative Timetables, by Fiscal Year

	2009	2010	2011	2012	2013	2014	Total, 2009–2014
	Average Number of U.S. Military Personnel in Iraq						
Administration's Plan[a]							
Withdraw 3 brigade equivalents per month, February 2010 through August 2010 and August 2011 through December 2011	140,000	95,500	47,500	2,500	0	0	n.a.
Alternative Timetables							
Option 1: Withdraw 4.1 brigade equivalents per month, October 2009 through June 2010[b]	140,000	42,500	0	0	0	0	n.a.
Option 2: Withdraw 5 brigade equivalents per month, October 2009 through May 2010[c]	140,000	34,000	0	0	0	0	n.a.
Option 3: Withdraw 5 brigade equivalents per month, February 2010 through September 2010[c]	140,000	76,500	0	0	0	0	n.a.
Option 4: Withdraw 1.6 brigade equivalents per month, February 2010 through December 2011[d]	140,000	111,500	47,000	1,500	0	0	n.a.
	Annual Cost (Billions of dollars in budget authority)						
Administration's Plan[a]	69	51	27	6	3	*	156
Alternative Timetables							
Option 1: Withdraw 4.1 brigade equivalents per month, October 2009 through June 2010[b]	69	27	7	2	0	0	106
Option 2: Withdraw 5 brigade equivalents per month, October 2009 through May 2010[c]	69	24	7	2	0	0	102
Option 3: Withdraw 5 brigade equivalents per month, February 2010 through September 2010[c]	69	41	7	4	0	0	122
Option 4: Withdraw 1.6 brigade equivalents per month, February 2010 through December 2011[d]	69	56	27	6	3	*	161
Memorandum:							
Costs for Activities Other than Operations and Equipment Reconstitution[e]	18	10	n.a.	n.a.	n.a.	n.a.	n.a.

Source: Congressional Budget Office.

Notes: OIF = Operation Iraqi Freedom; n.a. = not applicable; * = less than $500 million.

Numbers may not add to totals because of rounding. Costs for 2009 and for the Adminstration's plan for 2010 reflect actual budget requests. A brigade equivalent is considered to be a unit with an average of 3,500 military personnel equipped with approximately 1,000 military vehicles.

a. Withdrawal of about 10,500 U.S. military personnel per month.

b. Withdrawal of about 14,400 U.S. military personnel per month.

c. Withdrawal of about 17,500 U.S. military personnel per month.

d. Withdrawal of about 5,500 U.S. military personnel per month.

e. These activities include force protection, the Improvised Explosive Devices Defeat program, the Military Intelligence Program, Iraq security forces, coalition support, the Commander's Emergency Response Program, and military construction. The Administration could request additional budget authority in future years for those or other purposes, but CBO did not estimate those amounts.

The Administration's Plan for Withdrawal of U.S. Forces

In November 2008, Iraq and the United States signed an agreement stipulating that all U.S. military forces would be out of the country by the end of December 2011.[1] To meet that deadline, the United States must, by December 31, 2011, withdraw all of the roughly 140,000 military personnel that were in the country in March 2009. According to Administration officials, U.S. forces in Iraq decreased by roughly 10 percent to 128,000 service members by the end of September 2009 and are likely to remain at about that number to provide security for the elections in January 2010. President Obama announced that combat operations in Iraq would cease by the end of August 2010; after that, no more than 50,000 U.S. military personnel would remain in Iraq to train and advise Iraqi security forces, conduct counterterrorism operations, and provide force protection for remaining U.S. personnel.[2]

Using those waypoints as guides, CBO has estimated the number of U.S. troops that would stay in Iraq each month between September 2009 and January 2012—remaining at 128,000 through the election in January 2010, then dropping to 50,000 by the end of August 2010, and finally to zero by the end of December 2011 (see Figure 1). The highest rate of withdrawal under the Administration's plan will occur in the seven months from the beginning of February 2010 to the end of August 2010, when almost 80,000 U.S. military personnel will leave Iraq.[3] Another significant drawdown is scheduled for the end of calendar year 2011, when the remaining 50,000 U.S. troops will leave Iraq.

CBO estimates that, as forces are withdrawn, some of the annual costs associated with the war in Iraq could change from amounts requested for 2010. Not all funds that the Administration has requested for OIF—$61 billion in 2010—are related directly to the size of U.S. military forces there (all costs are presented in terms of budget authority).[4] Roughly $10 billion of the $61 billion was requested for items

---

1. Because the agreement covered U.S. military forces in Iraq and not those supporting Operation Iraqi Freedom from nearby countries (Kuwait, Qatar, Bahrain, and Saudi Arabia), this discussion concerns only the forces in Iraq. U.S. forces in the area surrounding Iraq have averaged about 20 percent of force levels in Iraq.

2. Catherine Dale, *Operation Iraqi Freedom: Strategies, Approaches, Results, and Issues for Congress,* CRS Report for Congress RL34387 (Congressional Research Service, April 2, 2009), p. 1, www.fas.org/sgp/crs/natsec/RL34387.pdf.

3. To some defense analysts, the term "plan" implies a detailed scheme for removing specific units on a specific timetable. In contrast, a "schedule" implies provision of broad guidance for withdrawal. In this discussion, CBO uses the terms "Administration's plan" and "Administration's schedule" interchangeably to refer to the broad outline that has been presented by the Administration for the withdrawal of U.S. troops from Iraq by the end of December 2011.

4. The request submitted by the Administration in May 2009 was intended to cover expenses for all of fiscal year 2010. In previous years, the Administration has requested supplemental funding later in the year.

Figure 1.

Withdrawal of U.S. Military Forces from Iraq Under the Administration's Plan

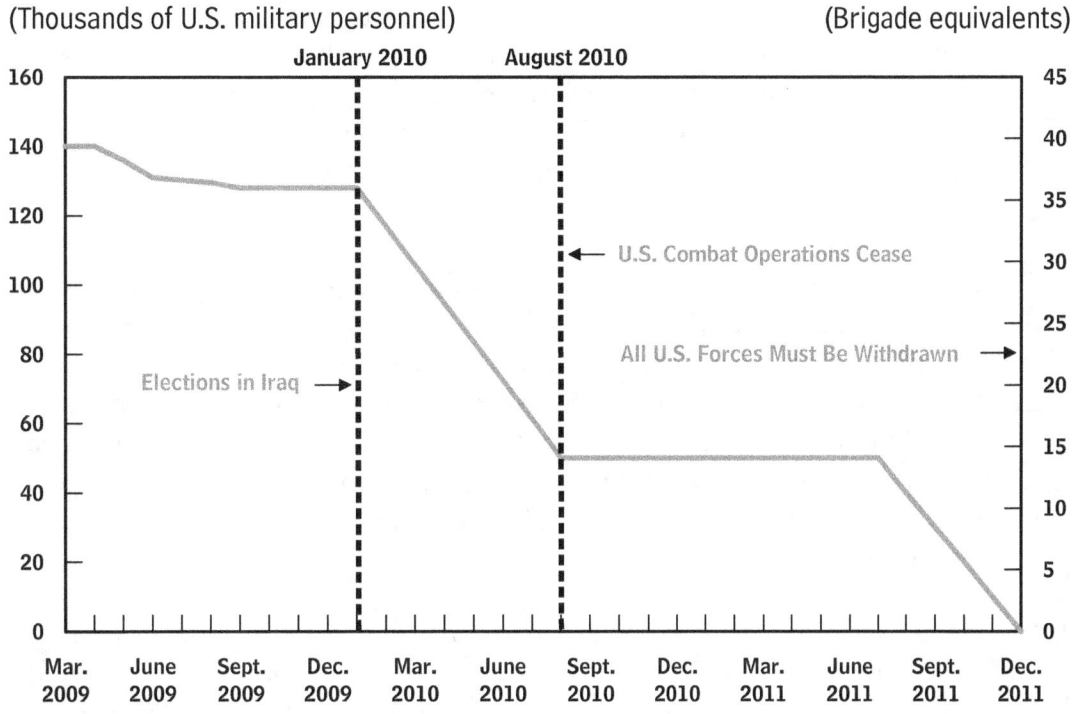

(Thousands of U.S. military personnel)　　　　　　　　　　　　　(Brigade equivalents)

Source: Congressional Budget Office.

Note: The actual numbers of military personnel are shown for March through September 2009; thereafter, the numbers are CBO's estimates.

or activities that are not necessarily tied to the number of U.S. military personnel in Iraq. For example, funds were requested for protective countermeasures for helicopters and intelligence capabilities. CBO concluded that funds for two categories—operations and equipment reconstitution—identified in the Administration's request for funds for OIF could be tied directly to the number of U.S. military personnel in Iraq. Those categories represent $51 billion, or 85 percent, of the $61 billion requested for 2010.[5] (See Appendix A for a discussion of costs associated with the war in Iraq, including a listing in Table A-1 of funds requested for 2009 and 2010. For a discussion of how the coming withdrawal might proceed and a brief review of two past U.S. withdrawals from the region, see Appendix B.)

---

5. CBO's estimates of the funds needed to support the war in Iraq after 2009 include only the amounts for operations and equipment reconstitution as defined by DoD. CBO's calculations did not include the costs for the Military Intelligence Program, force protection, the Commander's Emergency Response Program, the Defeat Improvised Explosive Devices program, or coalition support. Those costs totaled $10 billion in the 2010 request and might or might not decrease as U.S. military forces withdraw from Iraq.

As the number of U.S. military personnel in Iraq declines to zero by the second quarter of 2012, so too should the annual operations costs associated with those forces. On the basis of the Administration's schedule for withdrawal, CBO estimates that those costs would decrease after 2010 in proportion to the average number of U.S. military personnel in Iraq (see Appendix A, Table A-2). Even though all U.S. military forces are scheduled to be out of Iraq by the end of calendar year 2011, some U.S. military forces will remain behind for the first quarter of fiscal year 2012 (fiscal year 2012 begins October 1, 2011) and some residual operations costs will accrue—roughly $1 billion—for 2012. Thereafter, no significant annual costs should accrue for OIF operations.

DoD requested $9 billion in 2010 for "reconstitution"—replenishment, replacement, and repair—of equipment used in Iraq. As the United States reduces its forces in Iraq, costs for reconstitution also will decline, although more slowly. CBO anticipates that such costs could continue to accrue for two years after all U.S. forces are withdrawn from Iraq. CBO estimates that annual costs for repair and replacement of equipment used in Iraq would decline from $9 billion in 2010 to $3 billion in 2013 and to less than $500 million in 2014 (see Table A-2). Thereafter, CBO estimates, no further costs would be incurred.

When the two types of costs associated with OIF are combined, the total declines from $51 billion in 2010 to $27 billion in 2011 and to $6 billion in 2012, followed by a gradual decrease to less than $500 million in 2014 (see Table 1).

The Feasibility of Faster Schedules for Withdrawal

Several defense analysts and members of Congress have called for a faster end to the war in Iraq and for a quicker withdrawal of U.S. forces from that country. To determine what rates of withdrawal might be possible, CBO examined two instances within the past 20 years in which large numbers of U.S. military personnel were moved very quickly (see Appendix B).

However, there are some logistical constraints on how rapidly U.S. forces and their associated equipment and supplies can be withdrawn from Iraq and transported back to U.S. military bases. Another area of concern is the ability of the Iraqi government and its security forces to assume and maintain control of the political environment in Iraq, which also could slow the withdrawal of U.S. forces. CBO, however, did not examine in any detail how a more rapid drawdown would affect the political environment or security conditions in Iraq.

The Logistics of Removing U.S. Forces and Their Equipment from Iraq

To determine the scope of the task facing the military, CBO had to identify what must be moved from the theater, how to accomplish the move, and what assets would be available to do it.

Military Equipment to Be Removed from Iraq. Recent Army briefings and reports from the Government Accountability Office (GAO) and the RAND Corporation identify some likely challenges of withdrawing U.S. forces and associated equipment from Iraq.[6] Those documents list large quantities of military and contractor-operated equipment at hundreds of forward operating bases and thousands of tons of ammunition and supplies that potentially must be accounted for and transported out of Iraq. To minimize the amount of equipment and supplies that must be sent to bases in the United States and other countries, the Army and DoD plan to ship only what has potential military value for future operations—that is, equipment that is standard military issue and that is not worn out from use in Iraq. However, even if DoD succeeds in reducing the amount of supplies and nonmilitary equipment that must be transported home, removing military equipment will be a substantial undertaking.

According to the most recent data available to CBO, the United States had about 140,000 military personnel in Iraq as of March 2009. That translated to 14 brigade combat teams and their associated support units or to 40 brigade equivalents, 14 of which were combat brigades.[7] U.S. military forces in Iraq include a large number of personnel and large quantities of equipment—including vehicles, communications gear, generators, and supplies—that accompany and support the combat units.

CBO estimates that the United States had roughly 37 brigade equivalents in Iraq as of September 2009. Removing the equipment associated with those units from Iraq will require moving roughly 37,000 military vehicles—including trucks of all sizes and mine-resistant ambush-protected vehicles; almost 400 helicopters; and large quantities of communications gear, small arms, and medical equipment.[8] The equipment associated with forces in Iraq as of the fall of 2009 could weigh 750,000 tons and could fill between 37 and 74 large sealift ships.[9] In addition, transporting the roughly 13,500 tons of usable ammunition that might need to be removed from Iraq could require 3 additional ships in the strategic sealift fleet that are configured to carry ammunition. All told, in addition to 128,000 military personnel, and considering

---

6. Lieutenant General Mitchell Stevenson, "HQDA Logistics Update" (briefing to the Sustainment Commanders Conference, June 16, 2009); Government Accountability Office, *Operation Iraqi Freedom: Actions Needed to Enhance DoD Planning for Reposturing U.S. Forces from Iraq,* GAO-08-930 (September 2008), www.gao.gov/new.items/d08930.pdf; and Walter L. Perry and others, *Withdrawing from Iraq: Alternative Schedules, Associated Risks, and Mitigating Strategies* (report prepared by RAND Corporation for the Department of Defense, 2009), www.rand.org/pubs/monographs/MG882/.

7. A brigade combat team consists of 3,000 to 4,000 soldiers equipped with about 1,000 vehicles and, in some cases, an additional 300 or more armored vehicles, such as tanks and personnel carriers. (Although only the Army identifies units as brigade combat teams, CBO uses the term to refer to Army and Marine Corps combat units that include roughly the same number of personnel.) The term "brigade equivalent" is sometimes used to refer to any type of unit with an average of 3,500 military personnel and equipped with approximately 1,000 vehicles.

8. That estimate includes only standard military equipment assigned to military units.

9. One brigade equivalent's worth of equipment weighs roughly 20,000 tons, and transporting it requires one or two of the large ships the United States maintains in its strategic sealift fleet.

military assets only, up to 80 shiploads of material weighing more than 750,000 tons could need to be moved from Iraq to the United States, Europe, or South Korea.[10]

Moving Equipment from Iraq to the United States. The personnel and equipment in units leaving Iraq must first move to Kuwait to be processed for transport to home stations or other destinations in the United States. For Army equipment, which accounts for the bulk of U.S. military equipment in Iraq, the process can take 150 days from departure from the operating base in Iraq to arrival at a home station in the United States.

There are two points in the process that have been identified as limiting the number of vehicles—and therefore units—that can be shipped out of Kuwait each month. First, only one major highway from Iraq into Kuwait has been cleared for convoys, so border crossings are limited to a single point. The capacity of wash racks in the Kuwait staging area to clean vehicles before they are loaded onto ships presents a second constraint. (In contrast, the pier capacity of the commercial port in Kuwait and the deck capacity of the strategic sealift fleet's large ships are more than adequate to handle and transport many vehicles in a short time.)[11] Army estimates of the maximum capacity for removing units from Southwest Asia have cited the limits of three brigade equivalents per month for the road network and four brigade equivalents per month for the wash racks and customs inspections at the port in Kuwait.[12] As redeployment after Operation Desert Storm and in the early stages of Operation Iraqi Freedom demonstrated, however, the operation can move more rapidly. (Specific ways to alleviate some of the constraints are discussed under "Alternative Schedules for Withdrawal.")

Past Redeployments

Twice within the past 20 years the United States has withdrawn large numbers of U.S. forces from operations in Southwest Asia more quickly than constraints identified by the Army would indicate is possible (see Appendix B). The first was after Operation Desert Storm, when 130 brigade equivalents were removed in 4 months, for an average rate of 114,000 military personnel per month. The first rotation of U.S. forces in and out of Iraq, from December 2003 through May 2004, offers a more recent example: The equivalent of 37 brigades (a force equal to that in Iraq in September 2009) was returned home over 6 months—far shorter than the 30 months identified in the Administration's schedule. Thus, it is possible that people and equipment could be withdrawn from Iraq faster than the Army has estimated.

---

10. In making these estimates, CBO assumes that DoD will succeed in carrying out its plans to minimize the amount of material that needs to be transported out of Iraq (see Appendix B).

11. Each ship, which can carry at least half of a brigade equivalent's worth of equipment, can take three days to load.

12. The capacity of the road network is attributable in part to the need to provide security escorts for convoys, to the practice of loading U.S. military vehicles onto trucks for transit out of Iraq, and to the need to pass through the single border crossing into Kuwait.

That said, conditions in Iraq in 1991 and 2004 were different from the current situation. In neither case was it necessary for the United States to clean up and close forward operating bases. (In 1991, U.S. forces were not in Iraq long enough to establish such bases. In 2004, because U.S. forces were not leaving Iraq permanently, there was no need to close bases.) Moreover, after Operation Desert Storm and during the first OIF rotation, security measures currently used to protect convoys of U.S. military vehicles had not been instituted.

Alternative Schedules for Withdrawal

The two historical examples suggest it would be possible to withdraw U.S. military forces from Iraq more rapidly than the Administration has planned, although deteriorating security within Iraq or logistical complications might necessitate a slower withdrawal. CBO examined three schedules that would remove U.S. forces from Iraq more rapidly than the Administration's plan and one that would proceed more slowly. The first, Option 1, would have all forces withdrawn by the end of June 2010. Both Option 2 and Option 3 would withdraw 5 brigade equivalents per month, but each would begin and end on different dates—Option 2 would begin the withdrawal in October 2009 and conclude in May 2010; Option 3 would begin in February 2010, after the Iraqi elections in January 2010, and finish in September 2010. Under Option 4, U.S. forces would withdraw steadily over 23 months, beginning after the elections and concluding at the end of December 2011, a pace of withdrawal that is slower than under the Administration's plan. CBO has estimated the costs for operations and equipment reconstitution in OIF from 2010 through 2014 for each option.

CBO estimates that the costs of the withdrawal—for transporting equipment and personnel out of Iraq and for cleaning up and closing forward operating bases—would be essentially the same under the Administration's plan and the options discussed here. In each case, the amount of materiel removed and transported to its ultimate destination would be the same and the methods of transport would be the same, so there would be no difference in the cost.[13] Similarly, there is no difference in the number of forward operating bases that will need to be closed and cleaned up under the Administration's plan and under any option presented here.[14]

On the basis of redeployments in Operation Desert Storm and the early stages of OIF, and drawing from solutions proposed by various defense analysts, it seems plausible that the capacity of the road network and of facilities for cleaning vehicles could be

---

13. CBO estimates the cost to move 1 brigade equivalent's worth of materiel and personnel from Iraq to the United States to be roughly $50 million. (Personnel would move by air, equipment by sea.) The cost to move 37 brigade equivalents' worth from Iraq is included in CBO's estimates of the operations costs of OIF.

14. According to Army estimates, as of February 2009, the cost to clean up 65 forward operating bases in Iraq—9 large, 17 medium, and 39 small bases—would be $400 million to $750 million.

increased.[15] The rate at which U.S. units leave Iraq could be accelerated by any of several means:

- U.S. military vehicles (except for tracked vehicles) could be driven from Iraq to Kuwait, rather than loaded onto trucks,

- More wash racks could be built in Kuwait to process more vehicles per month, and

- More space could be obtained in Kuwait for storage of vehicles as they await shipment out of the area.

If military units leave Iraq before the bases at which they are stationed can be properly cleaned up and closed, it could be possible to leave skeleton crews and contractors to complete those tasks.

CBO estimates that the total increased cost to implement those measures—primarily to build more wash racks—would be less than $100 million.

Option 1: Withdraw All U.S. Military Forces by June 2010

One alternative CBO examined was the possibility of withdrawing all U.S. military forces from Iraq by the end of June 2010. If the withdrawal began in October 2009, 4.1 brigade equivalents—or 14,400 military personnel—would be removed each month, roughly 30 percent faster than during the most demanding portion of the Administration's schedule (see Figure 2). By withdrawing all U.S. forces by the end of June 2010, however, Option 1 would reduce the cost of operations and equipment reconstitution by about $50 billion from 2010 through 2014, mostly in 2010 and 2011 (see Table 1).

Ultimately, the rate of withdrawal and the amount of savings realized will depend on when the United States begins the withdrawal. If withdrawal begins after October 2009, the pace must increase and savings relative to the Administration's plan will decrease if the June 2010 deadline is to be met (see Table 2). If the United States does not begin the withdrawal until November 2009, the pace will need to rise to 4.6 brigades (16,000 military personnel) per month. And because more U.S. forces would be in Iraq longer, CBO estimates, the costs of operations and equipment reconstitution from 2009 through 2014 would increase by $2.5 billion (and the savings

---

15. Lawrence J. Korb, Sean E. Duggan, and Peter M. Juul, *How to Redeploy: Implementing a Responsible Drawdown of U.S. Forces from Iraq* (Washington, D.C.: Center for American Progress, updated August 2008), pp. 14–18, www.policyarchive.org/handle/10207/7757; and Perry and others, *Withdrawing from Iraq*, pp. 44–47.

Figure 2.

Withdrawal of U.S. Military Forces from Iraq Under the Administration's Plan and Option 1

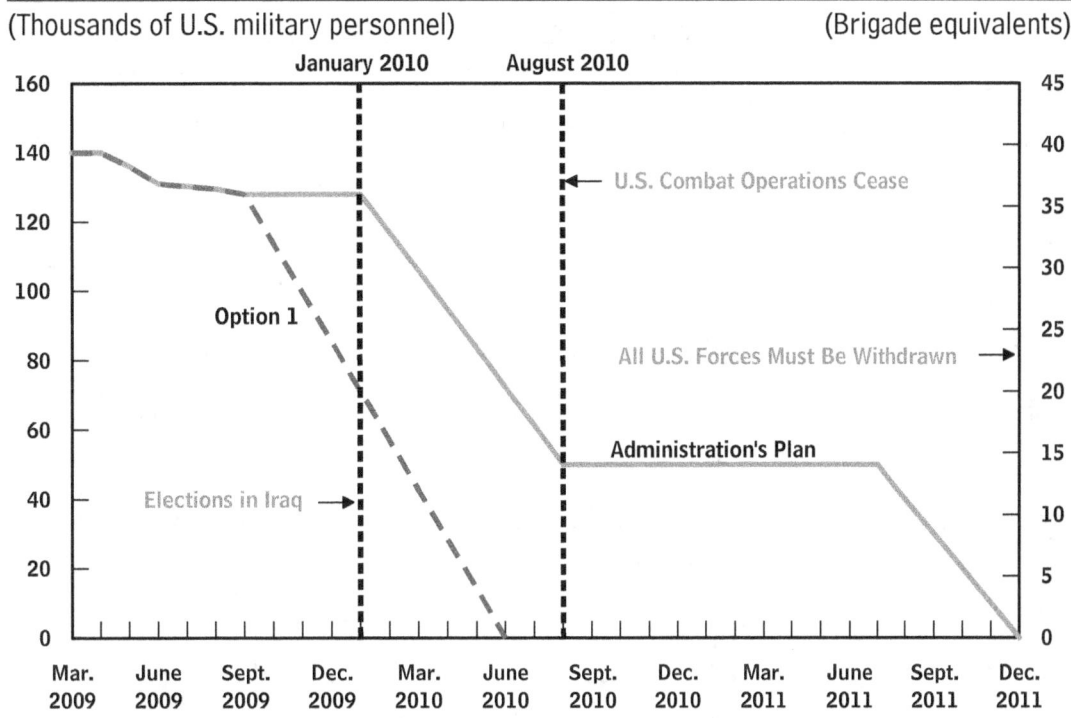

(Thousands of U.S. military personnel)　　　　　　　　　　　　　　(Brigade equivalents)

Source:　Congressional Budget Office.

Note:　The actual numbers of military personnel are shown for March through September 2009; thereafter, the numbers are CBO's estimates.

compared with the Administration's plan would fall from $50 billion to $48 billion). If the start of withdrawal is delayed past the beginning of December 2009, the rate required to withdraw all U.S. forces by June 2010 would exceed 5 brigade equivalents per month, and each month's delay would reduce savings by $2.5 billion.

Options 2 and 3: Withdraw U.S. Forces at a Rate of Five Brigade Equivalents per Month

CBO examined the implications of withdrawing U.S. forces from Iraq at 5 brigade equivalents—or roughly 17,500 service members—per month, a rate similar to that recommended by the Center for American Progress.[16] Withdrawal at that rate would be faster than at any time under the Administration's scheduled drawdown, but it would be slower than the movement of U.S. forces out of Kuwait after Operation Desert Storm or during the early rotations of OIF. CBO considered two start dates for the withdrawal of U.S. forces: Option 2 would begin in October 2009 and Option 3

16.　Korb, Duggan, and Juul, in *How to Redeploy*, recommended withdrawing 140,000 U.S. military personnel over 8 to 10 months. The options described here would require 8 months but start with slightly fewer personnel.

Table 2.

Effect of Various Starting Dates on Troop Withdrawal and Savings for Option 1

	Withdrawal Rate (Brigade equivalents per month)	Savings from Administration's Plan (Billions of dollars)
October 2009	4.1	50
November 2009	4.6	48
December 2009	5.2	46
January 2010	6.1	43
February 2010	7.3	41

Source: Congressional Budget Office.

Note: Under Option 1, all U.S. military personnel would be withdrawn from Iraq by June 2010. A brigade equivalent is considered to be a unit with an average of 3,500 military personnel equipped with approximately 1,000 military vehicles. Savings are in budget authority over the period from 2009 through 2014.

would begin after Iraq's elections in January 2010. In each case, withdrawal would be completed 8 months later, in May 2010 for Option 2 and in September 2010 for Option 3 (see Figure 3).

The largest savings compared with the Administration's plan would be achieved by pursuing Option 2, initiating a rapid drawdown in October 2009. CBO estimates that option would produce savings of $54 billion from 2009 through 2014. Fully half—$27 billion—would be realized in 2010. The costs under that timetable would be slightly less than the costs under Option 1.

However, starting the withdrawal of troops before the elections scheduled for January 2010, and doing so rapidly, would raise the risk of undermining the stability of the country at a politically difficult time. If withdrawal was delayed until after the elections, the cost would be higher but still about $34 billion less than under the Administration's plan (see Table 1).

Disadvantages of Withdrawing Troops Faster than Under the Administration's Plan

Withdrawing U.S. forces faster than planned by the Administration could cause difficulties that CBO has not quantified. Among the areas of concern are the availability of adequate facilities and services for returning U.S. military personnel and for demobilizing and processing returning reservists. During the early stages of OIF, the press reported on substandard temporary housing for U.S. military personnel returning from Iraq and awaiting medical treatment. An assessment of those problems is not within CBO's areas of expertise, but some observers assert that such problems could exist for several months as DoD processes large numbers of returning military personnel.

Figure 3.

Withdrawal of U.S. Military Forces from Iraq Under the Administration's Plan and Options 2 and 3

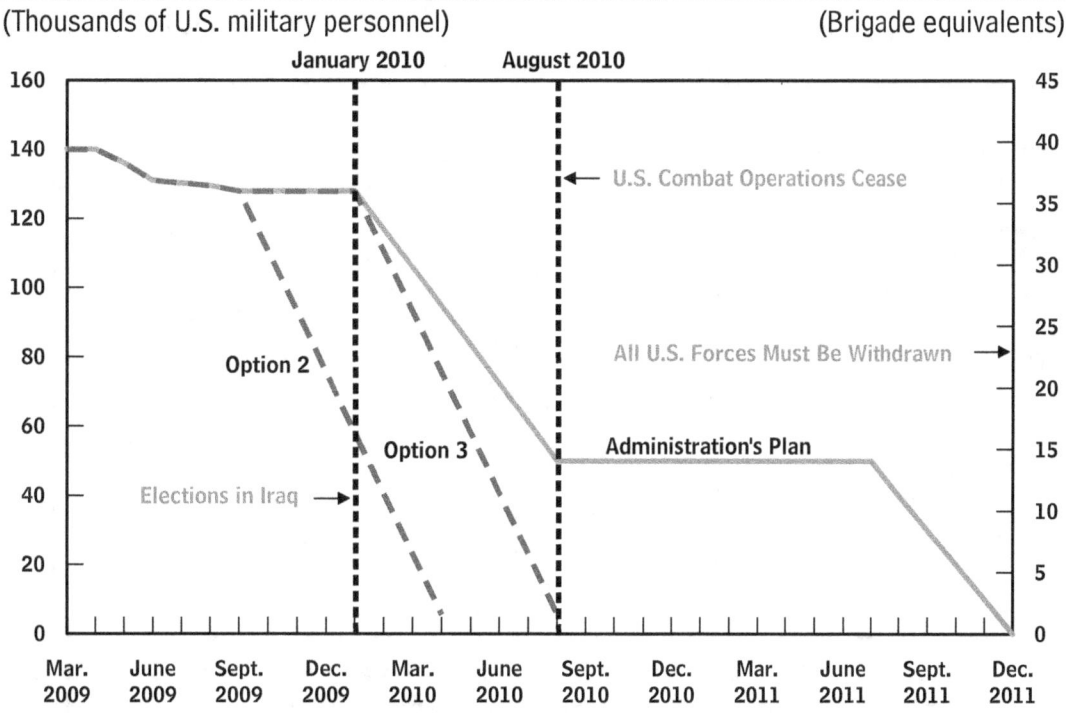

(Thousands of U.S. military personnel)　　　　　　　　　　　　　(Brigade equivalents)

Source:　Congressional Budget Office.

Note:　The actual numbers of military personnel are shown for March through September 2009; thereafter, the numbers are CBO's estimates.

Security concerns also have been identified as areas for consideration in assessing alternative plans for removing vehicles from Iraq or closing forward operating bases. To avoid creating more U.S. military targets, the current practice is to place U.S. military vehicles on commercial flatbed trucks or on military trucks driven out of Iraq by contractors. If U.S. soldiers drive from Iraq to Kuwait there is a greater—and potentially unacceptable—risk of exposure to attack. Similar concerns have been raised about the security of U.S. forces remaining in Iraq to clean up and close forward operating bases if most military personnel have already left. Although it is possible for skeleton crews to oversee contractors who might complete the process, those crews could be without adequate protection in the face of a threat.

A final area of concern involves a possible lack of planning time and the inability to fully account for equipment if its departure from Iraq is rushed. GAO and RAND emphasized that orderly withdrawal requires thorough planning and scheduling of departures.[17] Without adequate time to plan, to monitor arrivals and departures of U.S. military equipment at the port in Kuwait, and to label all equipment in transport, the arrival of each piece of equipment on schedule at its appropriate destination

---

17.　See Government Accountability Office, *Operation Iraqi Freedom*; and Perry and others, *Withdrawing from Iraq*.

Figure 4.

Withdrawal of U.S. Military Forces from Iraq Under the Administration's Plan and Option 4

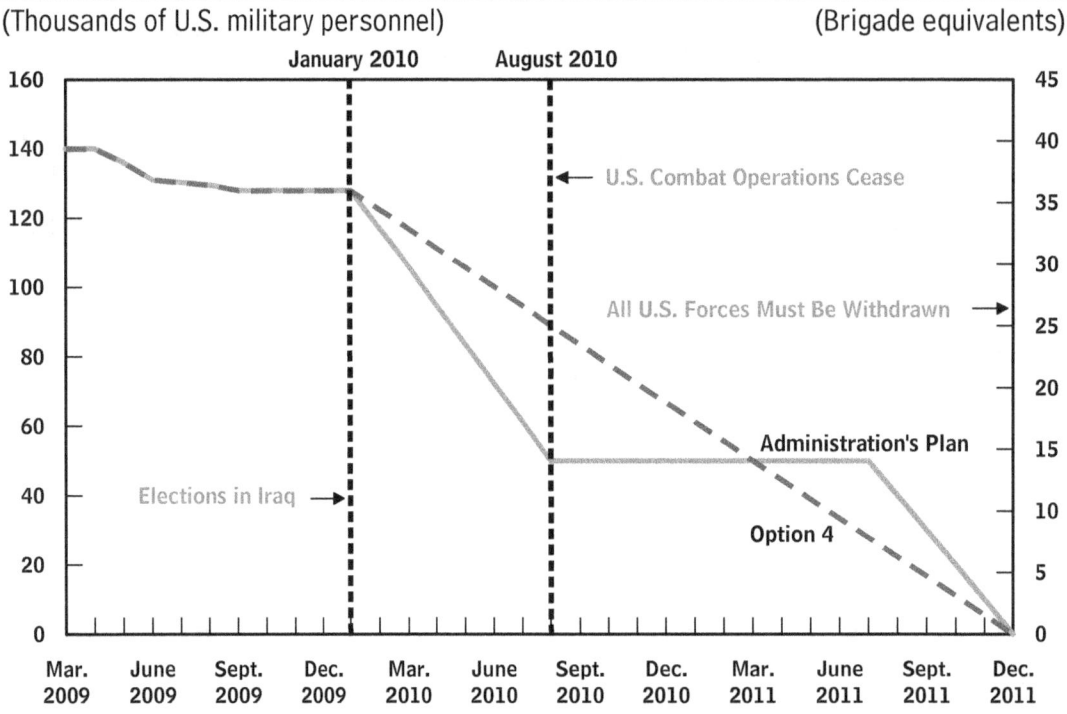

(Thousands of U.S. military personnel)   (Brigade equivalents)

Source: Congressional Budget Office.

Note: The actual numbers of military personnel are shown for March through September 2009; thereafter, the numbers are CBO's estimates.

is not assured. Similar concerns were raised following the rapid withdrawal of U.S. forces from Southwest Asia after Operation Desert Storm.[18]

Option 4: Withdraw U.S. Military Forces More Slowly than Under the Administration's Plan

The security considerations and potential logistical complications discussed above might cause the Administration to withdraw forces from Iraq more slowly than it currently plans. Therefore, CBO analyzed an option that would withdraw U.S. forces at a steady rate of 1.6 brigade equivalents—or about 5,500 personnel—per month beginning immediately after the Iraqi elections and concluding at the end of December 2011. Such a plan would maintain a larger presence from February 2010 through March 2011 than the Administration's plan now foresees (see Figure 4). By CBO's estimates, the costs would be about $5 billion more than the corresponding costs for OIF under the Administration's plan and almost $60 billion more than the costs under Option 2 (see Table 1).

---

18. See General Accounting Office, *Operation Desert Storm: Lack of Accountability Over Materiel During Redeployment,* GAO/NSIAD-92-258 (September 1992, p. 3), http://archive.gao.gov/d35t11/147771.pdf.

Appendix A:
Costs Associated with
Operation Iraqi Freedom

In its analysis, the Congressional Budget Office (CBO) compared actual or estimated costs for operations and equipment reconstitution for Operation Iraqi Freedom (OIF) for the period from 2009 through 2014 under the Administration's plan and for several alternatives. The Administration's full request for funds for 2009 and 2010 was examined by functional category, and CBO estimated costs for operations and equipment reconstitution for 2010 through 2014.

Categories of Funds Requested for Operation Iraqi Freedom in 2009 and 2010

Funds requested by the Department of Defense (DoD) for the war in Iraq for 2009 and 2010 are divided into several categories (see Table A-1), which DoD defined in summary justification materials that accompanied its budget request for fiscal year 2010. (Those categories do not correspond to appropriations titles used in the department's annual "Green Book" to describe its budget requests).[1]

CBO's Estimates of Costs Related to U.S. Military Forces in Iraq

CBO estimated the costs for two categories that could be related directly to the number of U.S. military personnel in Iraq—operations and equipment reconstitution—for the Administration's plan from 2011 through 2014 and for alternative withdrawal timetables for 2010 through 2014.

Operations Costs

Operations costs include incremental costs for military personnel and costs for operation and maintenance (O&M) associated with U.S. forces conducting the war in Iraq.[2]

---

1. See Department of Defense, *Fiscal Year 2010 Budget Request Summary Justification* (May 2009, pp. 4-1 to 4-54 and 5-17 to 5-20), www.defenselink.mil/comptroller/defbudget/fy2010/fy2010_SSJ.pdf; and Department of Defense, *National Defense Budget Estimates for FY 2010* (June 2009), www.defenselink.mil/comptroller/defbudget/fy2010/Green_Book_Final.pdf.

2. "Operations" includes activities listed in the Department of Defense's request for funds for overseas contingency operations. See Department of Defense, *Fiscal Year 2010 Budget Request Summary Justification,* pp. 4-10 to 4-15.

Table A-1.

Categories of Funds Requested for OIF for 2009 and 2010

(Billions of dollars)

	2009	2010
Operations	52.4	41.9
Equipment Reconstitution	16.5	9.4
Force Protection	9.6	7.4
Improvised Explosive Devices Defeat Program	2.7	0.8
Military Intelligence Program	3.2	1.0
Iraq Security Forces	1.0	0
Coalition Support	0.4	0.1
Commander's Emergency Response Program	0.7	0.3
Military Construction	0.1	0
Total	**86.5**	**60.8**

Source: Congressional Budget Office based on Department of Defense, *Fiscal Year 2010 Budget Request Summary Justification* (May 2009), p. 5-19.

Notes: OIF = Operation Iraqi Freedom.

Numbers may not add to totals because of rounding. Amounts shown are for budget authority requested for the fiscal year.

Incremental Military Personnel Costs. Incremental military personnel costs include special pay and benefits for deployed military personnel, such as combat pay; food served in dining facilities and rations for deployed personnel; and full-time pay for activated reservists. Military personnel costs should be directly related to the number of U.S. forces in Iraq and to the number of military personnel outside Iraq directly supporting OIF. In estimating annual incremental personnel costs for the war in Iraq, CBO assumed that the number of U.S. military personnel deployed in Southwest Asia outside of Iraq directly involved in supporting the war will decrease in proportion to the drawdown of U.S. military forces in Iraq. As a consequence, CBO estimates that overall annual military personnel costs associated with the war will decrease proportionately with the drawdown of U.S. forces in Iraq.

Operation and Maintenance Costs. CBO also estimates that costs for operation and maintenance included in the Administration's "operations" category would decline as forces are withdrawn. O&M expenses include fuel and spare parts for equipment in military units and for transportation of personnel and equipment to and from Iraq; contract labor in Iraq to feed, house, and guard U.S. forces there; and maintenance and repair of military equipment such as Stryker vehicles and the large number of high mobility multipurpose wheeled vehicles. O&M funds also pay for the activities of civilian and contractor personnel in areas surrounding Iraq and in the United States to the extent that they support the war in Iraq.

CBO estimates that the O&M costs per service member would increase no faster than the overall rate of inflation during the remainder of the U.S. military involvement in

OIF. From 2003 through 2007, the per-person O&M costs of overseas contingency operations increased faster than general inflation from year to year.[3] Since 2007, however, O&M costs and the number of U.S. military personnel involved in overseas contingency operations—including both Iraq and Afghanistan—have remained relatively constant.

CBO estimates that the costs associated with contractors supporting the war also would decline in proportion to the decrease in U.S. military forces in Iraq. This relationship should remain valid even if the costs associated with some types of contractors increased as the military presence in Iraq declined. For example, the number of contractor personnel supporting OIF decreased from 133,000 in March 2009 to 120,000 in June 2009 as the U.S. military presence in Iraq declined. Nevertheless, the number of private security contractors hired by the Department of Defense to provide security at specific sites increased from 10,700 to 13,200 over the same period.[4] Although that trend runs counter to CBO's overall assumption, the size of the contract for the private security forces (with annual obligations of about $250 million) is not large enough to reverse the overall trend that the size and cost of contractor support decreases as the number of U.S. military personnel in Iraq declines.

Total Costs of Operations in OIF. Separate costs for DoD's operations category for the war in Iraq have been identified only for fiscal years 2009 and 2010. Before that, the information available covers combined operations costs for all overseas contingencies. Those combined costs have remained relatively constant, after adjusting for inflation, as the number of personnel involved in overseas contingencies also has remained relatively stable. However, the funds requested by DoD for operations for OIF for 2009 and 2010 do not decrease proportionately with the planned reduction in personnel involved, even after adjusting for inflation. Nevertheless, when estimating costs associated with the war in Iraq for years after 2010 for the Administration's plan and after 2009 for alternative timetables, CBO assumed that the cost of operations would decline in proportion to the number of U.S. military personnel in Iraq, after adjusting for inflation. (See Table A-2 for CBO's estimates of operations costs under the Administration's plan and the four options.)

Equipment Reconstitution Costs

"Equipment reconstitution" includes three broad categories: replenishing expendable items, such as ammunition and missiles; replacing equipment—such as helicopters

---

3. See Congressional Budget Office, "Analysis of the Growth in Funding for Operations in Iraq, Afghanistan, and Elsewhere in the War on Terrorism," letter to the Honorable Kent Conrad (February 11, 2008).

4. See Walter Pincus, "With U.S. Forces in Iraq Beginning to Leave, Need for Private Guards Grows," *Washington Post* (September 8, 2009), www.washingtonpost.com/wp-dyn/content/article/2009/09/07/AR2009090702242.html.

Table A-2.

Annual Costs of Operations and Equipment Reconstitution in OIF Under the Administration's Plan and Alternative Timetables, by Fiscal Year

(Billions of dollars in budget authority)

	2009	2010	2011	2012	2013	2014	Total, 2009–2014
Administration's Plan: Withdraw 3 Brigade Equivalents Per Month, February 2010 Through August 2010 and August 2011 Through December 2011[a]							
Operations	52	42	20	1	0	0	115
Equipment reconstitution	17	9	7	5	3	*	41
Total[b]	69	51	27	6	3	*	156
			Alternative Timetables				
Option 1: Withdraw 4.1 Brigade Equivalents Per Month, October 2009 Through June 2010[c]							
Operations	52	18	0	0	0	0	70
Equipment reconstitution	17	9	7	2	0	0	36
Total	69	27	7	2	0	0	106
Option 2: Withdraw 5 Brigade Equivalents Per Month, October 2009 Through May 2010[d]							
Operations	52	14	0	0	0	0	67
Equipment reconstitution	17	9	7	2	0	0	35
Total	69	24	7	2	0	0	102
Option 3: Withdraw 5 Brigade Equivalents Per Month February 2010 Through September 2010[d]							
Operations	52	32	0	0	0	0	84
Equipment reconstitution	17	9	7	4	0	0	37
Total	69	41	7	4	0	0	122
Option 4: Withdraw 1.6 Brigade Equivalents Per Month February 2010 Through December 2011[e]							
Operations	52	47	20	1	0	0	120
Equipment reconstitution	17	9	7	6	3	*	42
Total	69	56	27	6	3	*	161

Source: Congressional Budget Office.

Notes: OIF = Operation Iraqi Freedom; * = less than $500 million.

Numbers may not add to totals because of rounding. Costs for 2009 and for the Administration's plan for 2010 reflect actual budget requests. A brigade equivalent is considered to be a unit with an average of 3,500 military personnel equipped with approximately 1,000 vehicles.

a. Withdrawal of about 10,500 U.S. military personnel per month.

b. The Administration requested $18 billion in 2009 and $10 billion in 2010 in budget authority for items other than operations and equipment reconstitution, including force protection, the Improvised Explosive Devices Defeat program, the Military Intelligence Program, Iraq security forces, coalition support, the Commander's Emergency Response Program, and military construction. The Administration could request additional budget authority in future years for those or other purposes, but CBO did not estimate those amounts.

c. Withdrawal of about 14,400 U.S. military personnel per month.

d. Withdrawal of about 17,500 U.S. military personnel per month.

e. Withdrawal of about 5,500 U.S. military personnel per month.

and trucks—that has been destroyed or severely damaged; and repairing and restoring equipment returning from Iraq to its predeployment condition. The cost for equipment reconstitution is related both to the number of military personnel conducting operations in Iraq and to the amount of equipment returning to home stations. As U.S. forces are withdrawn, the number of missiles and the amount of ammunition expended; the number of aircraft, trucks, and other items destroyed; and the quantity of equipment being returned to home stations in any one year also should decline.

But the requirement for funds to replace and repair equipment is not likely to fall as quickly as the withdrawal occurs, for several reasons. Requests for funds to replace equipment cannot be made until after the equipment is destroyed, and it could take until the next fiscal year to put in a request to replace a piece of equipment. Similarly, requests to replace expended munitions generally are made on the basis of the prior year's expenditures, and it can take a full year to make such requests. Finally, repair costs could accrue for as long as two years after forces are withdrawn because it can take up to six months after a unit has left Iraq for its equipment to reach the home station or a repair depot. In addition, significant amounts of some types of equipment used in Iraq, such as trucks, remain there for use by replacement units.[5] Thus, some equipment could remain in Iraq or Kuwait after all major U.S. forces have left Iraq, awaiting shipment back to the United States.[6] For all of those reasons, CBO estimates that costs for repair and replacement of equipment used in Iraq will decrease as the number of U.S. military personnel in Iraq declines, although with a delay of two years. (See Table A-2 for CBO's estimates of equipment reconstitution costs under the Administration's plan and the four alternative timetables.)

---

5. All helicopters and almost all major weapons, such as tanks, Bradley fighting vehicles, and Stryker vehicles, return to their home stations when their associated units leave Iraq.

6. The Army asserts that costs to repair and replenish its equipment would continue for at least two years after all U.S. forces are removed from Iraq.

Appendix B:
The Process of Withdrawing
U.S. Forces from Iraq

The complex process of withdrawing U.S. forces and their associated equipment from Iraq is examined in this appendix. In addition to establishing specific processes for returning personnel and equipment, the Department of Defense (DoD) also has identified ways to minimize the amount of materiel that must be removed from Iraq and transported to the United States. Two instances from the past 20 years provide examples of occasions on which DoD has returned large numbers of U.S. military personnel and equipment to the United States in relatively short periods of time.

Withdrawing Personnel and Equipment

Once a unit in Iraq is designated for withdrawal from the country, the troops and equipment must make their way to staging areas in Kuwait. Depending on where the unit is stationed, that can take up to three days. During the move, all vehicles are loaded onto trucks driven by contractors.[1] All U.S. Army convoys have military escorts for security and all of them use a single designated route out of Iraq to Kuwait. One last constraint is the sole checkpoint at the Iraq–Kuwait border. Those considerations, according to one Army estimate made in the fall of 2008, limit the pace of units exiting Iraq to three brigade equivalents—or roughly 10,500 troops—per month.

After all elements of a unit have arrived at the staging area in Kuwait, the equipment is prepared for shipment to the United States, Europe, or South Korea—a process that can take from 30 to 50 days. During that time, equipment is accounted for, identified with a unit, and labeled for transport to its destination. All equipment is washed and sterilized so that no pathogens are transported out of the country. After inspection and clearance by customs officials and employees of the U.S. Department of Agriculture, the equipment is transferred to sterile yards to await loading onto ships.

From then on, equipment and personnel take separate paths to their destinations. Personnel from the unit fly from Kuwait City International Airport back to a home station, and transport ships generally set off with the equipment for ports in the continental United States. After arrival at U.S. ports—about a month after leaving Kuwait—the equipment is loaded onto railcars for transport to Army depots or the unit's home station for repair. The time elapsed between the equipment's arrival in a port and at its ultimate destination can be another three weeks.

---

1. Heavy equipment with tracks, such as tanks, is moved on transporters that are too wide to pass one another on the main highway leading from the Kuwait border to the staging area.

Disposition of Equipment

To minimize the amount of materiel that must shipped from Iraq to the United States, Europe, or South Korea, DoD plans the following actions, as appropriate:[2]

- Supplies and ammunition in Iraq as of the summer of 2009 would be consumed in Iraq; shipments of supplies into Iraq from outside the country would slow in anticipation of the planned drawdown.

- Equipment that can be deployed in Afghanistan or used to replenish the Army's prepositioned stocks either in Kuwait or at sea would be transferred to the appropriate location rather than transported back to the United States.[3]

- Equipment currently in Iraq that the United States deems no longer useful—for example, some of the thousands of armored high mobility multipurpose wheeled vehicles purchased early in the war and subsequently replaced by mine-resistant ambush-protected vehicles—would be sold to other countries, such as Iraq, for use by their armies.

- Equipment that is not standard military issue—including computers, telephones, equipment for gyms built at forward operating bases, and some 30,000 vehicles purchased by the U.S. government but operated by contractors—would be sold or donated to the Iraqi government or other DoD-approved recipients.[4]

Past Withdrawals of U.S. Forces from Southwest Asia

Two examples from the past 20 years demonstrate that the rapid withdrawal of large numbers of U.S. military personnel and their equipment is possible.

Return from Operation Desert Storm

Both the buildup and the drawdown of U.S. forces in Southwest Asia associated with Operation Desert Storm were substantial and rapid. During the 6 months before February 1991, the United States transported 500,000 military personnel and more

---

2. Lieutenant General Mitchell Stevenson, "HQDA Logistics Update" (briefing to the Sustainment Commanders Conference, June 16, 2009); Government Accountability Office, *Operation Iraqi Freedom: Actions Needed to Enhance DoD Planning for Reposturing U.S. Forces from Iraq*, GAO-08-930 (September 2008), www.gao.gov/new.items/d08930.pdf; Michael Cervone, "Drawdown and Redistribution Policy Guidance for Major End Items" (information brief to the Army Reserve Forces Policy Committee, May 18, 2009); Fawzia Sheikh, "Pentagon Likely to Remove Most U.S. Gear from Iraq in Coming Years," *Inside the Army* (March 23, 2009); and Michelle Tan, "Drawdown of 2.8 Million Pieces of Equipment May Cost Tens of Billions," *Army Times* (August 24, 2009), p. A18.

3. To speed the response of U.S. military units in the event of a crisis, the Army stores equipment in Kuwait, at other locations around the world, and on ships.

4. The vehicles that contractors use but that are owned by the U.S. government include pickup trucks, sport utility vehicles, and trailers that are not standard military vehicles.

than 4 million tons of supplies and equipment to Saudi Arabia and surrounding areas.[5] At the end of the operation, when the ceasefire had been signed, almost twice as much time—11 months from March 1991 through January 1992—was needed to remove roughly the same amount of equipment from the area.[6]

Because the United States had not built any operating bases in Kuwait and had agreed with Saudi Arabia that there would be no American presence in that country after the conflict, the U.S. military leadership determined to withdraw military personnel from the theater as quickly as possible.[7] In the first month after the ceasefire, about 165,000 military personnel were flown home; another 200,000 military personnel went home in the next two months. Using the brigade equivalent (3,500 people) as a guide, those rates of redeployment translate to 35 brigade equivalents per month with a surge rate of 47 brigade equivalents in the first month.

The pace of removal of equipment and supplies, although not as rapid, nevertheless was relatively fast. To accelerate the removal of equipment from Kuwait, wash rack capacity near the ports in Kuwait after Operation Desert Storm was increased to 2,000 vehicles—or 2 brigade equivalents—per day. (This compares with the current estimated surge capacity of 4 brigade equivalents per month.) Almost 130,000 vehicles were cleaned and shipped out of the theater in four months, for an extended rate of removal of 33 brigade equivalents per month. The large stocks of ammunition were the last materiel to be removed from the theater. Over nine months, 320,000 tons of ammunition—more than 20 times the amount currently estimated to be in Iraq—was cleaned, packaged, and removed from the theater.

First Rotation In and Out of Iraq for Operation Iraqi Freedom

The first rotation of U.S. forces occurred over the six months from December 2003 through May 2004. During that exchange, about 130,000 U.S. military personnel—representing 37 brigade equivalents—and their associated equipment left the theater and returned to their home stations.[8] That exchange of troops represented the removal of 6 U.S. brigade equivalents per month.

---

5. David Kassing, "Getting U.S. Military Power to the Desert: An Annotated Briefing," RAND Note N3-508/AF/A/OSD (prepared for the Department of Defense, 1992), www.dtic.mil/cgi-bin/GetTRDoc?AD=ADA428172&Location=U2&doc=GetTRDoc.pdf.

6. Lieutenant General William G. Pagonis and Jeffrey L. Cruikshank, *Moving Mountains: Lessons in Leadership and Logistics from the Gulf War* (Boston: Harvard Business School Press, 1992).

7. Ibid., p. 156.

8. Lawrence J. Korb, Sean E. Duggan, and Peter M. Juul, *How to Redeploy: Implementing a Responsible Drawdown of U.S. Forces from Iraq* (Washington, D.C.: Center for American Progress, updated August 2008), p. 7, www.policyarchive.org/handle/10207/7757.